Fun & Easy Way To Draw Manga Animals

Zoo Art: Your Handy Guide to Drawing Manga Animals

How to Draw Manga Animals

By: Gala Publication

Published By:

Gala Publication
ISBN-13: **978-1522802549**
ISBN-10: **1522802541**

©Copyright 2015 – Gala Publication

INDEX

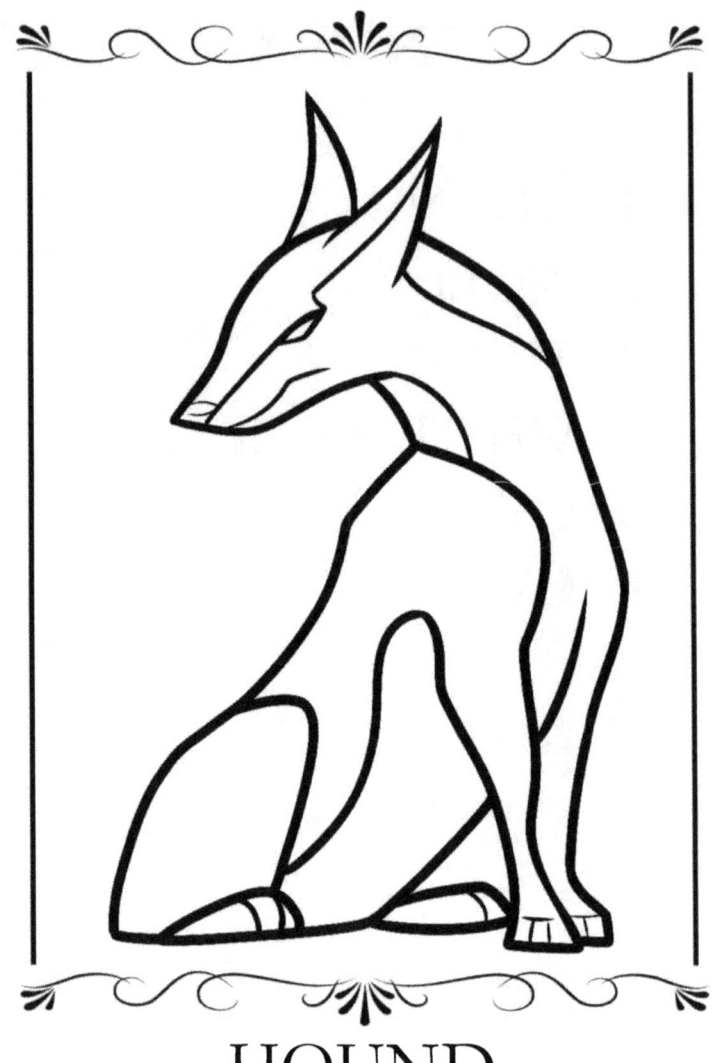

HOUND

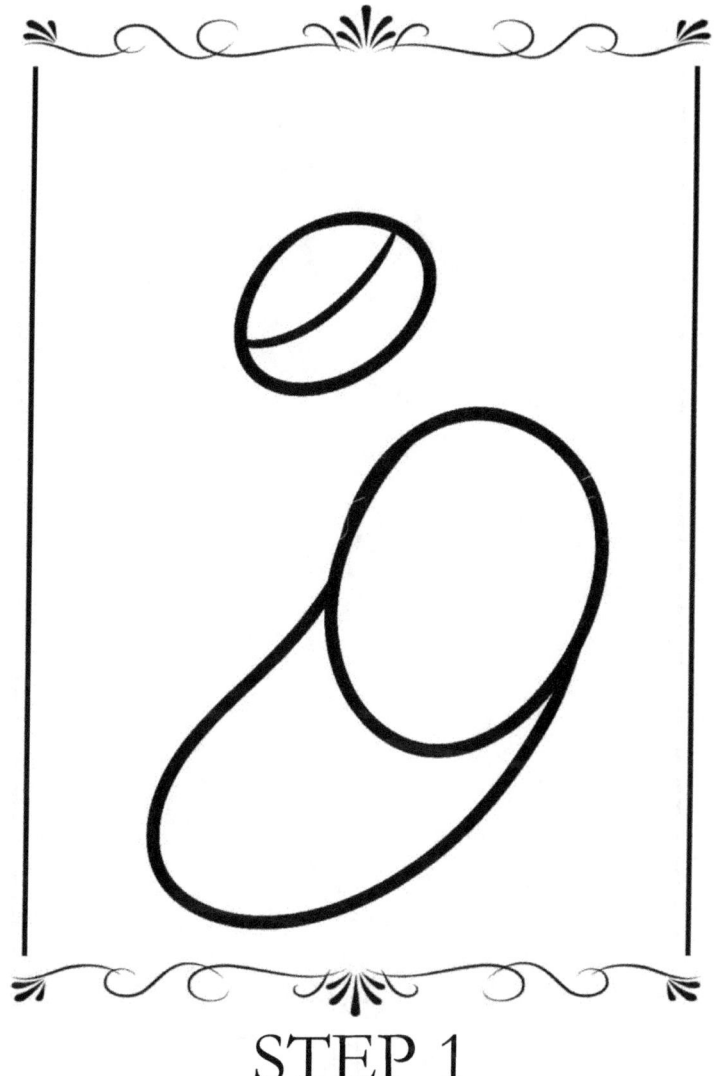

STEP 1

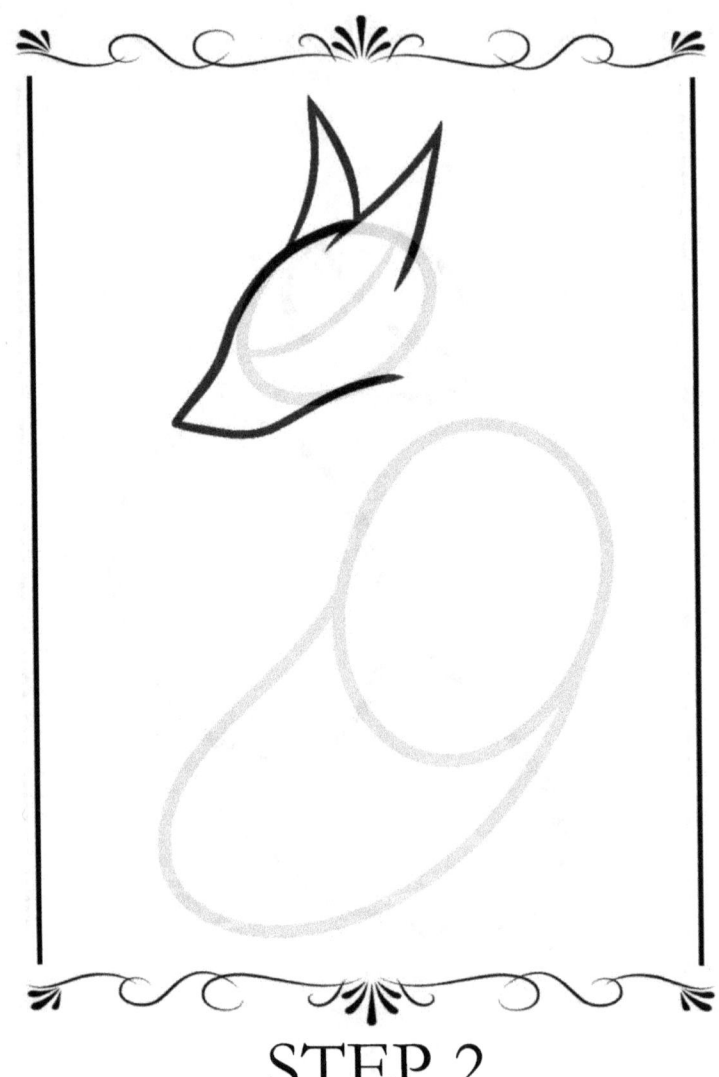

STEP 2

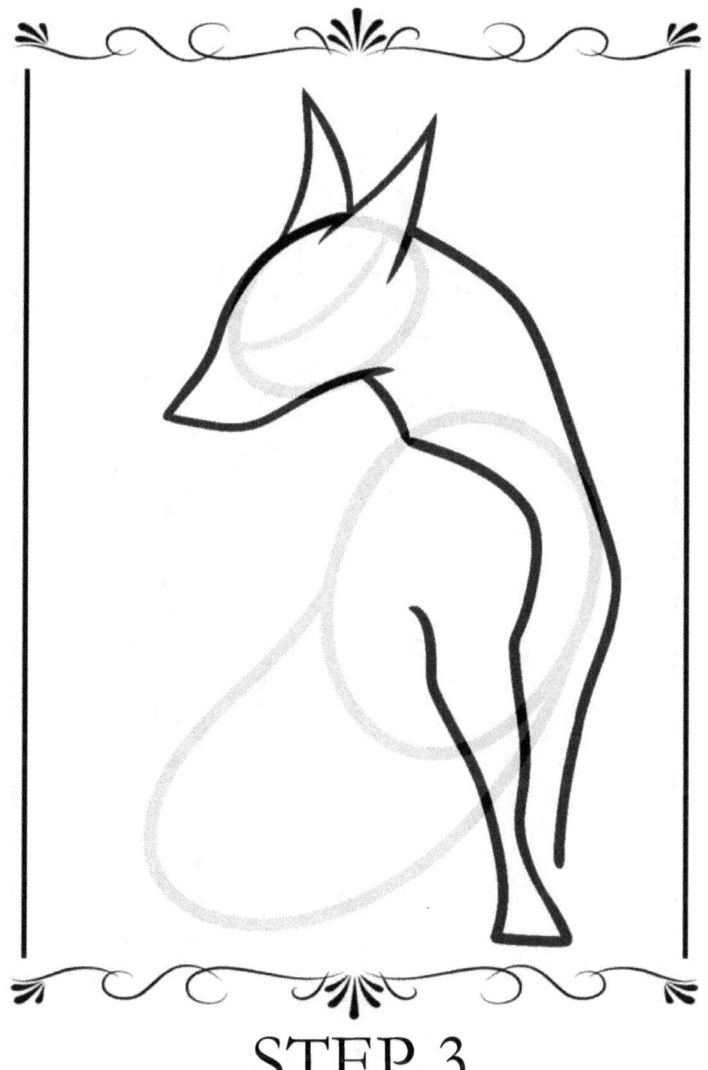

STEP 3

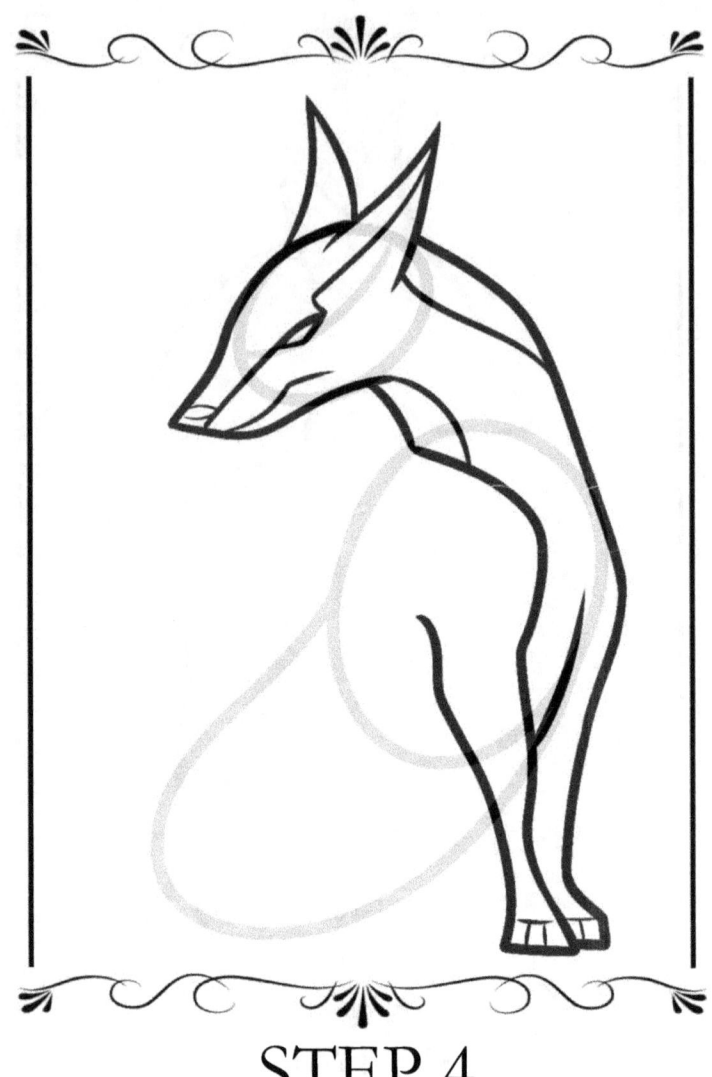

STEP 4

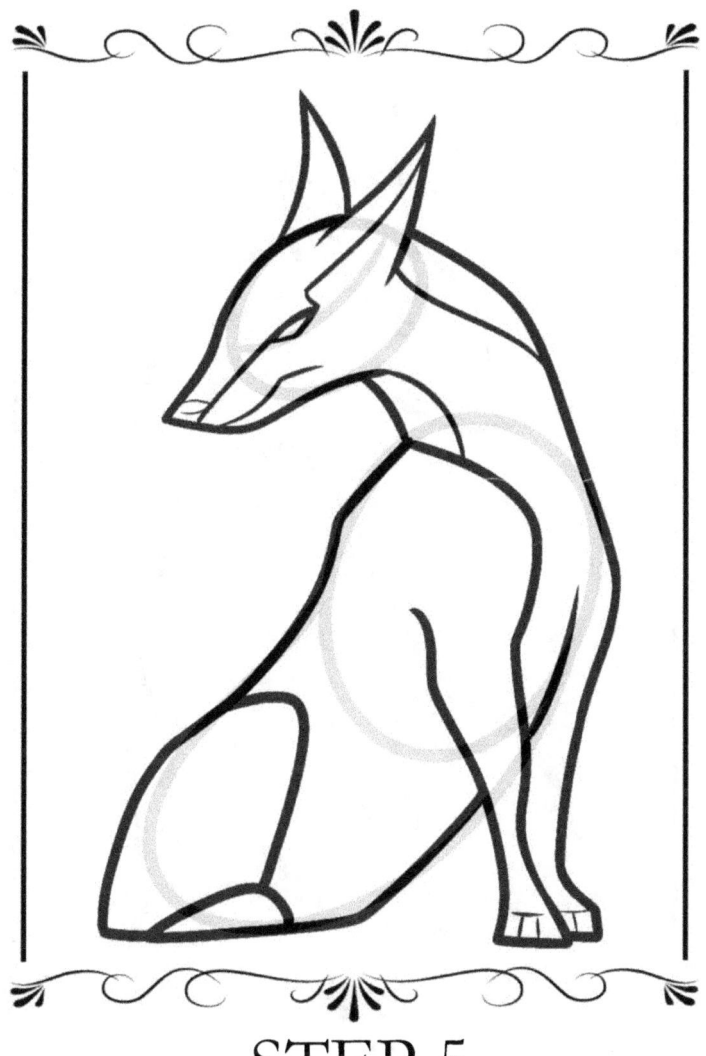

STEP 5

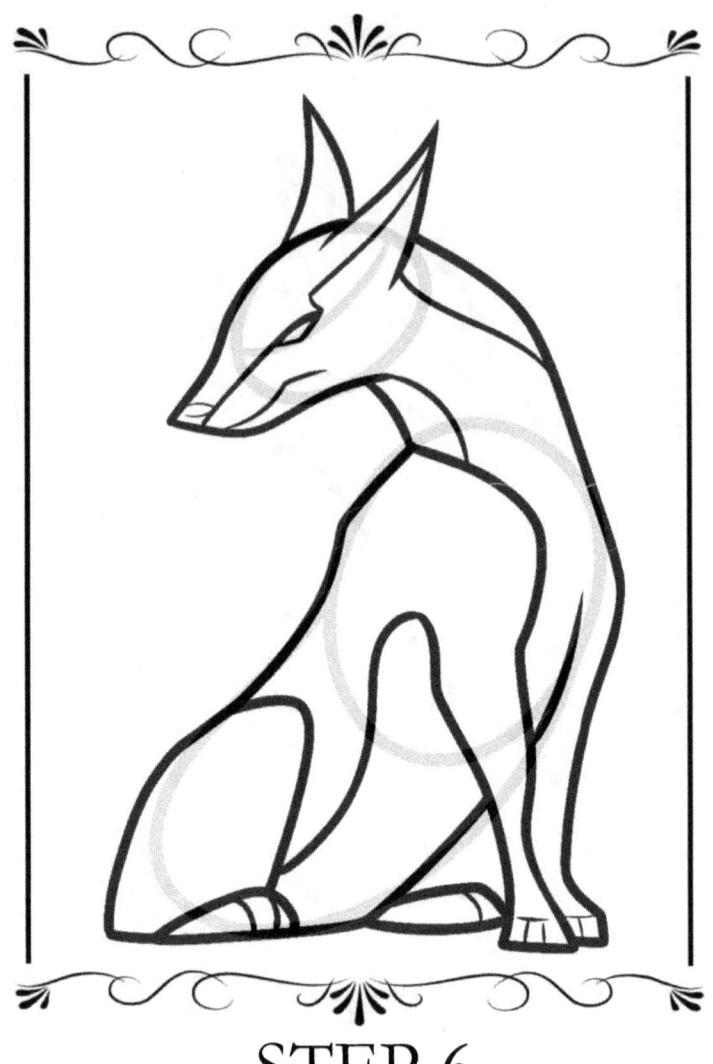

STEP 6

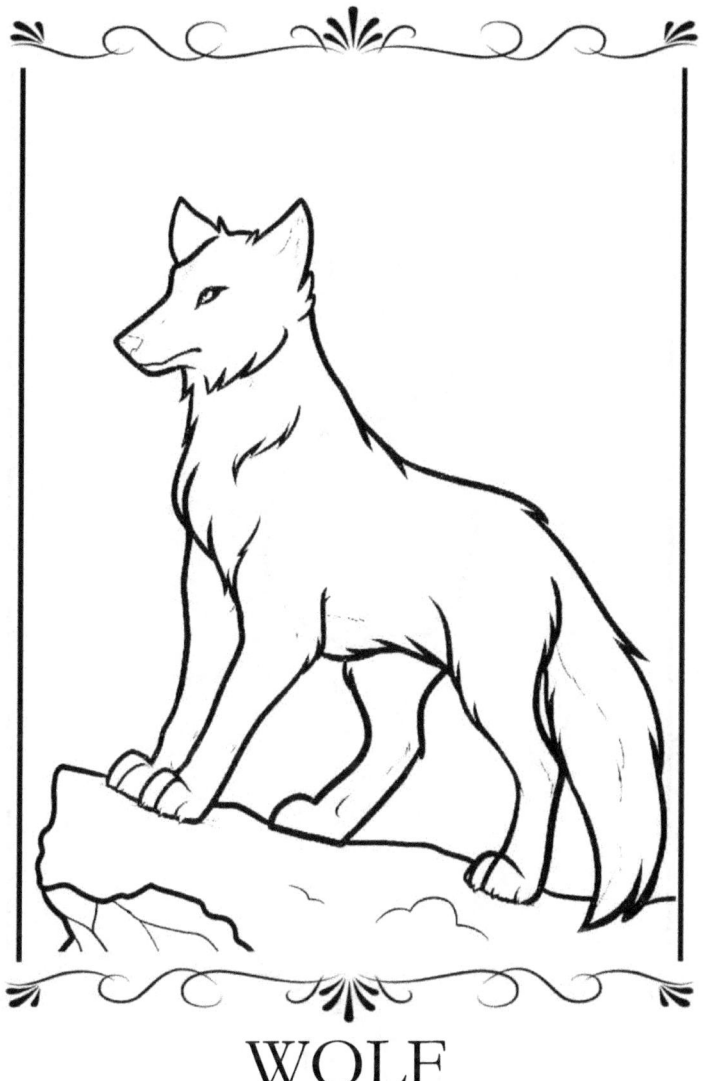

WOLF

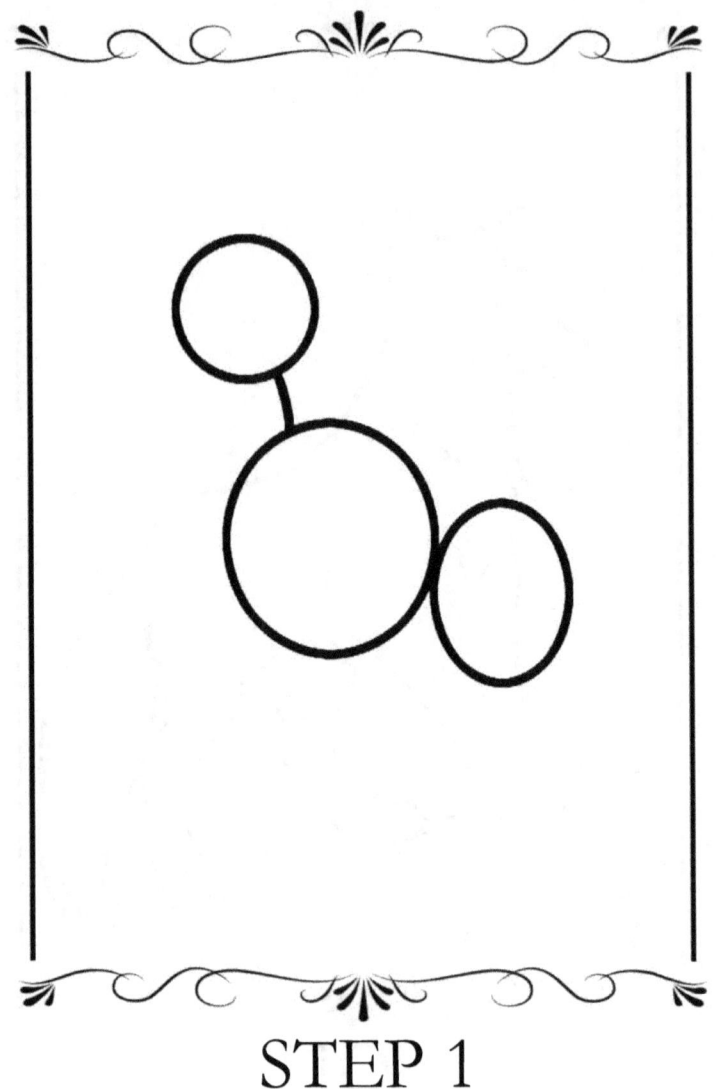

STEP 1

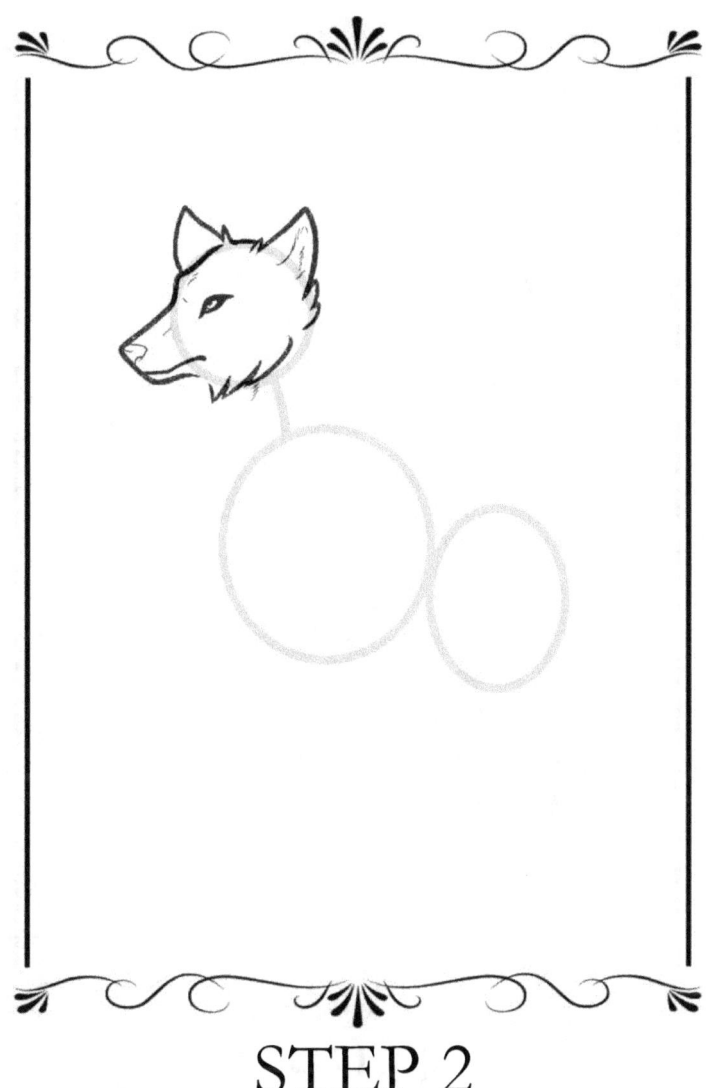

STEP 2

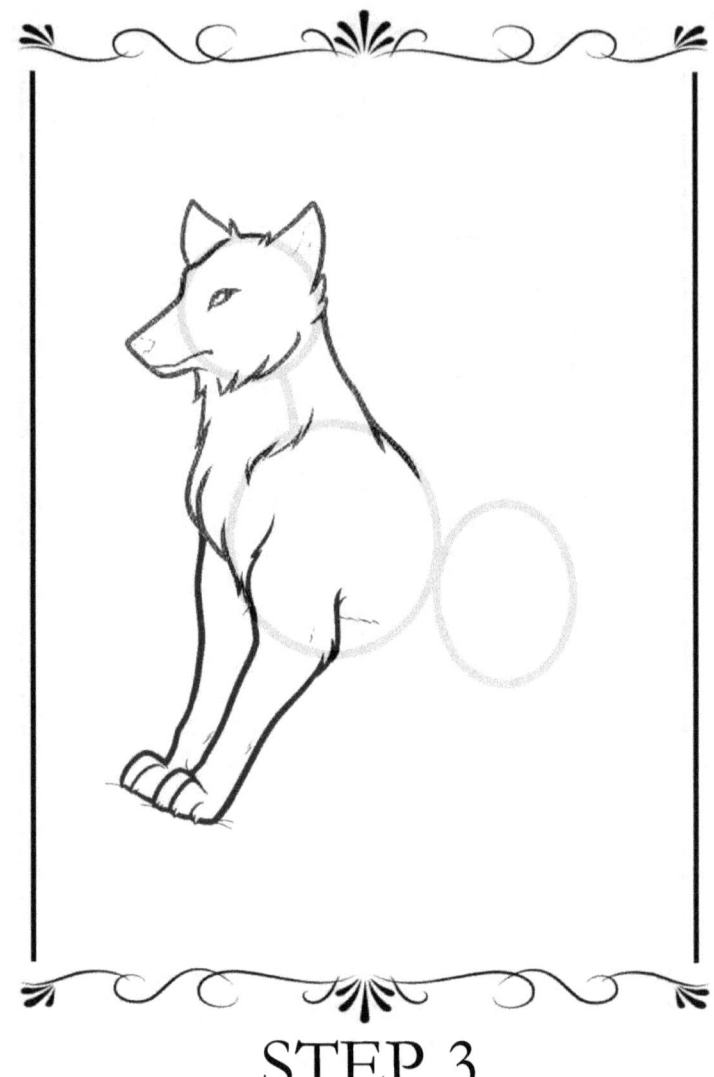

STEP 3

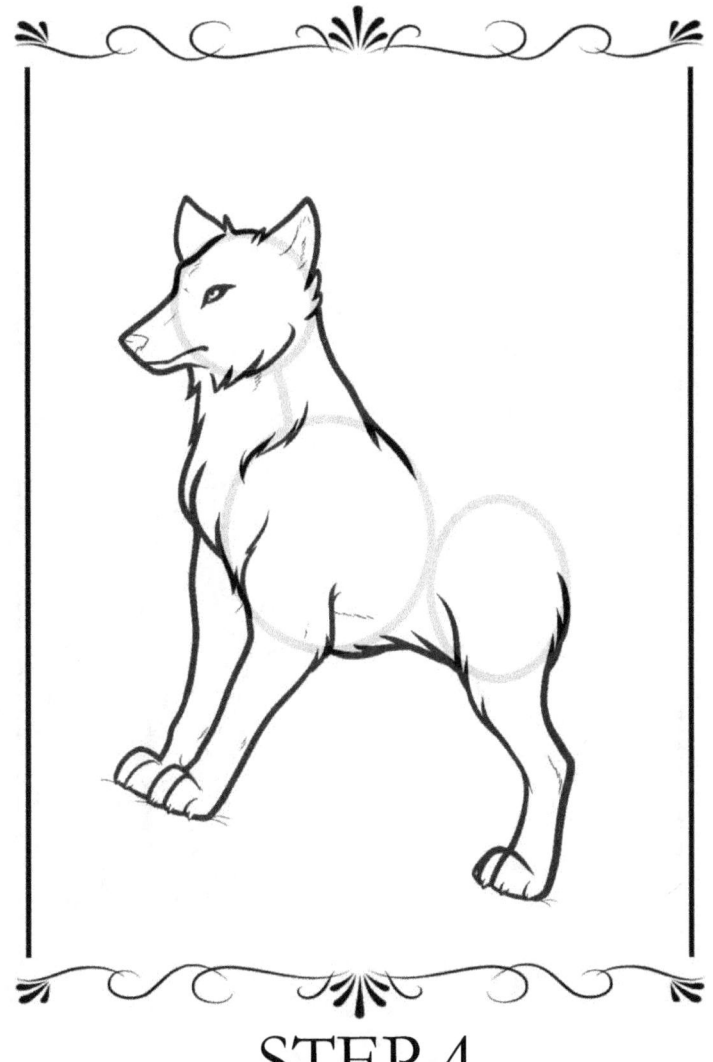

STEP 4

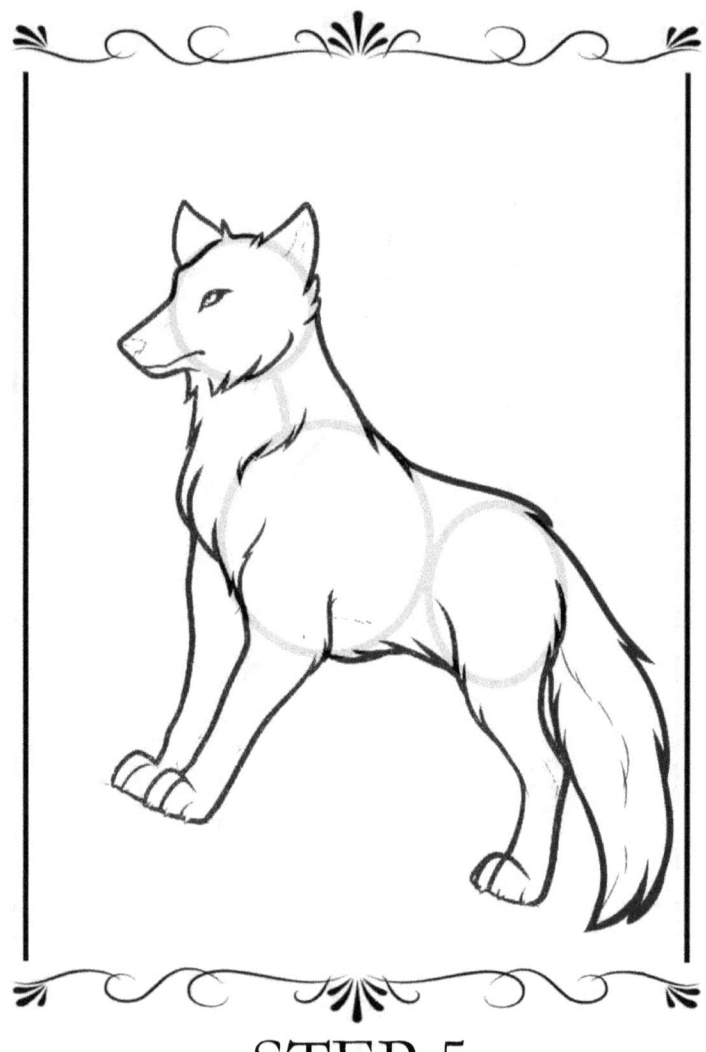

STEP 5

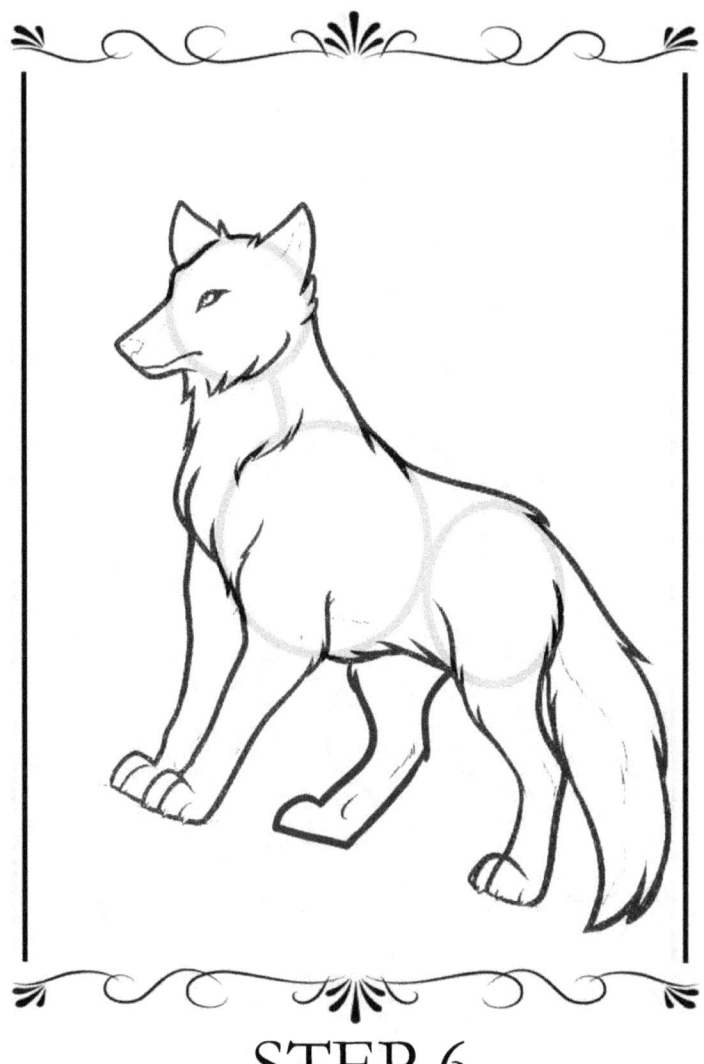

STEP 6

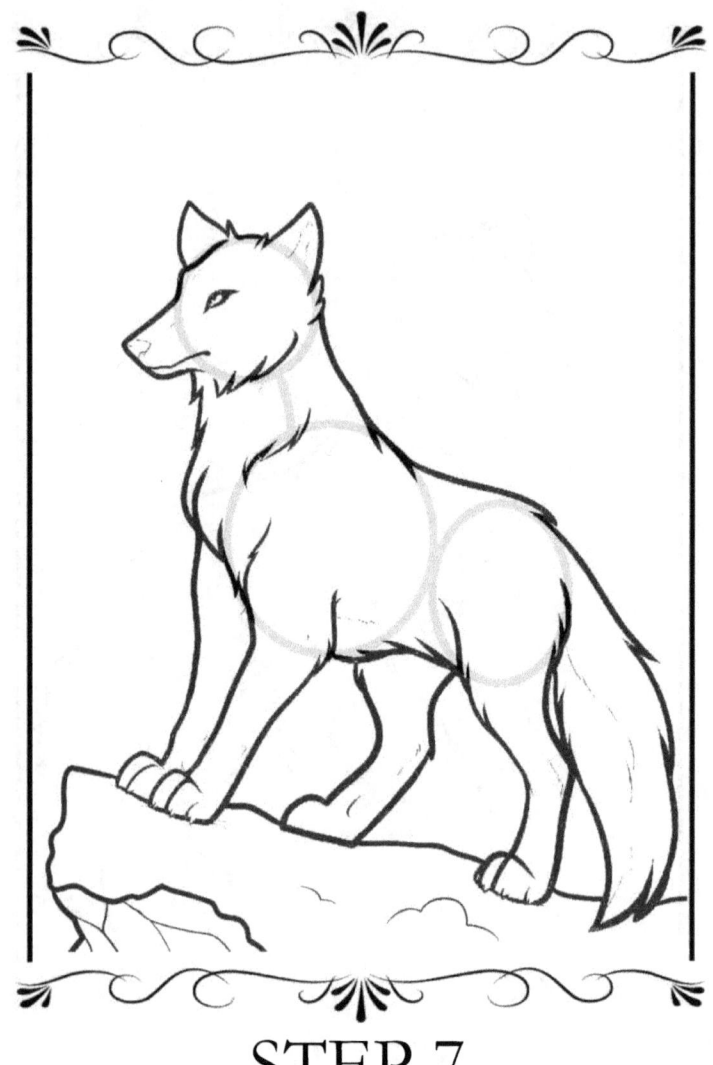

STEP 7

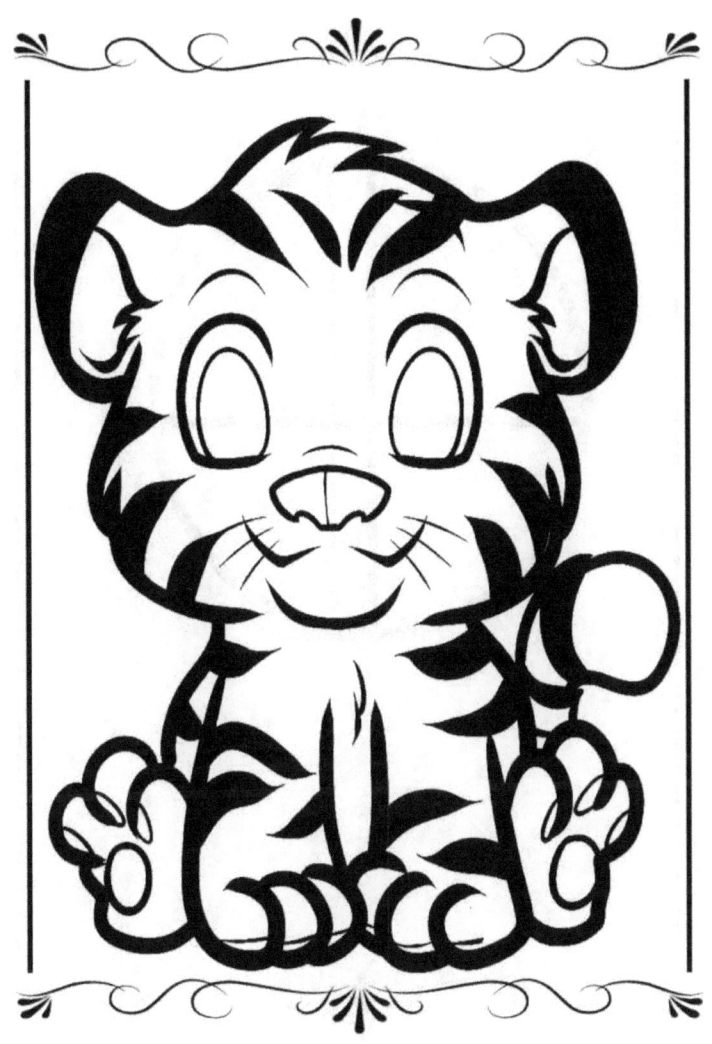

TIGER

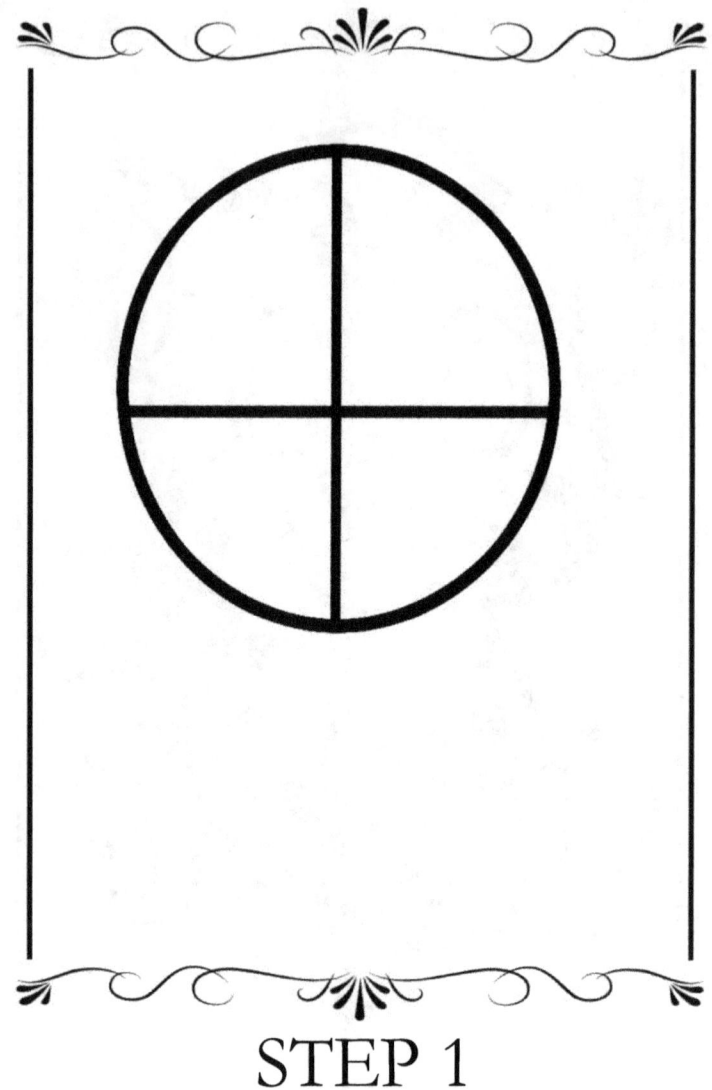

STEP 1

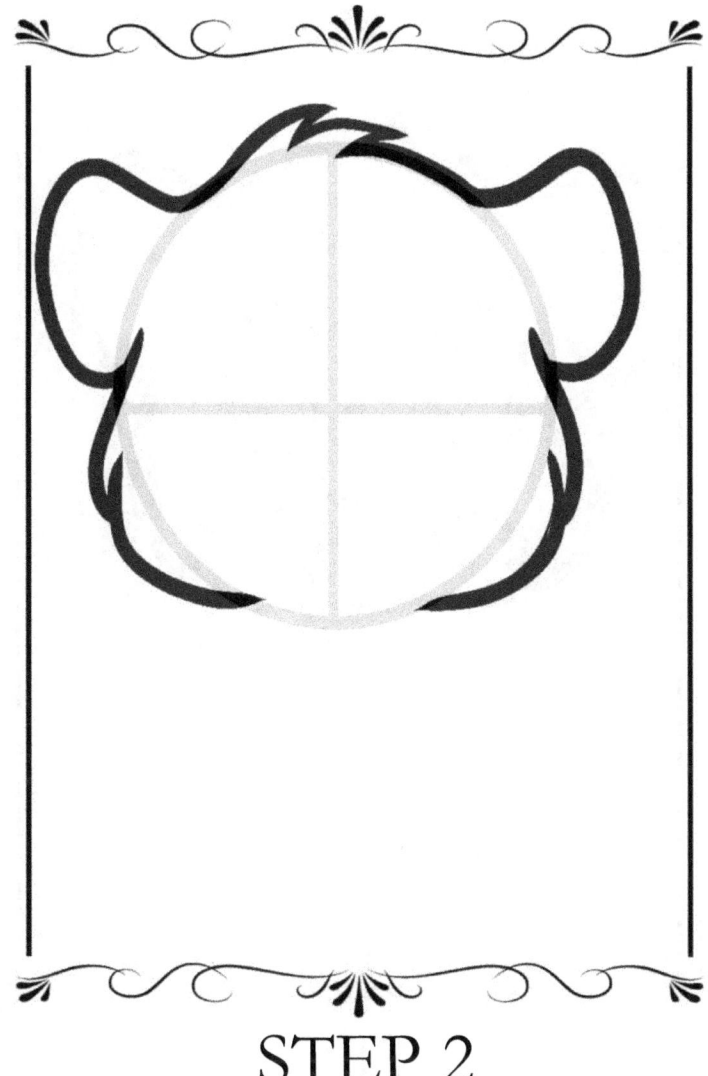

STEP 2

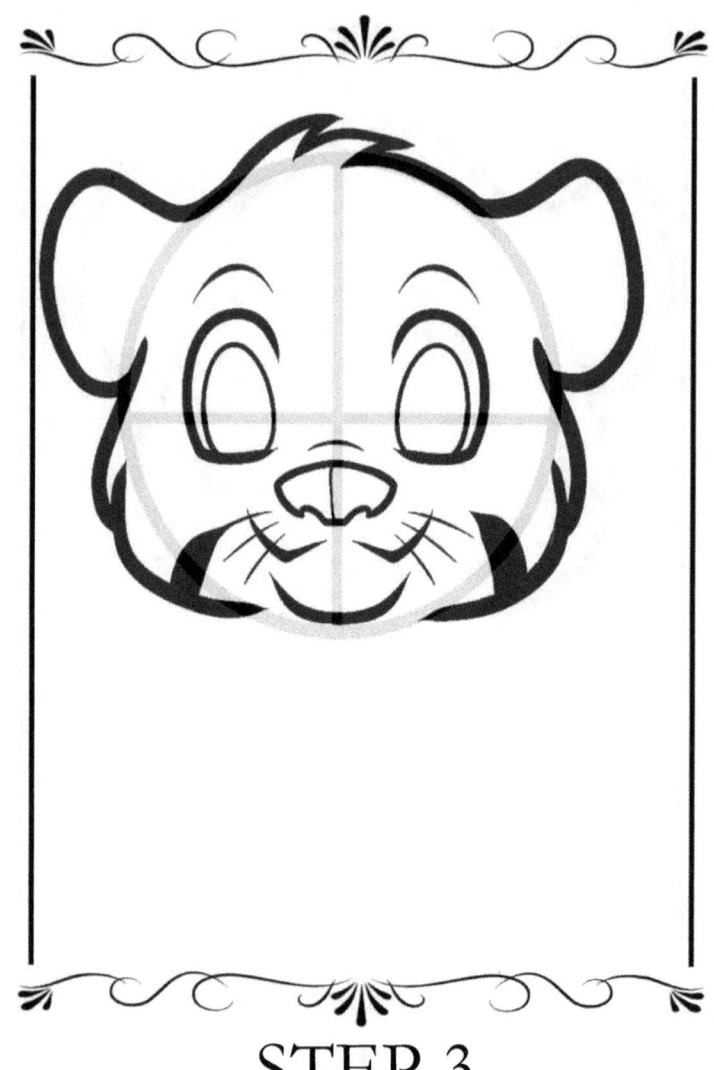

STEP 3

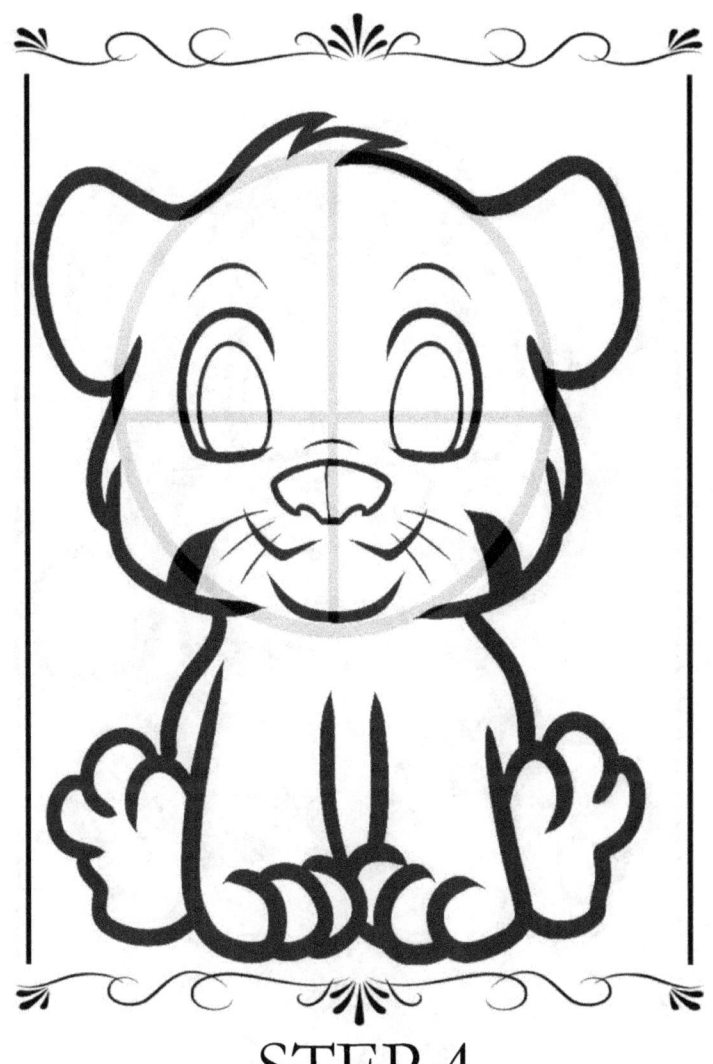

STEP 4

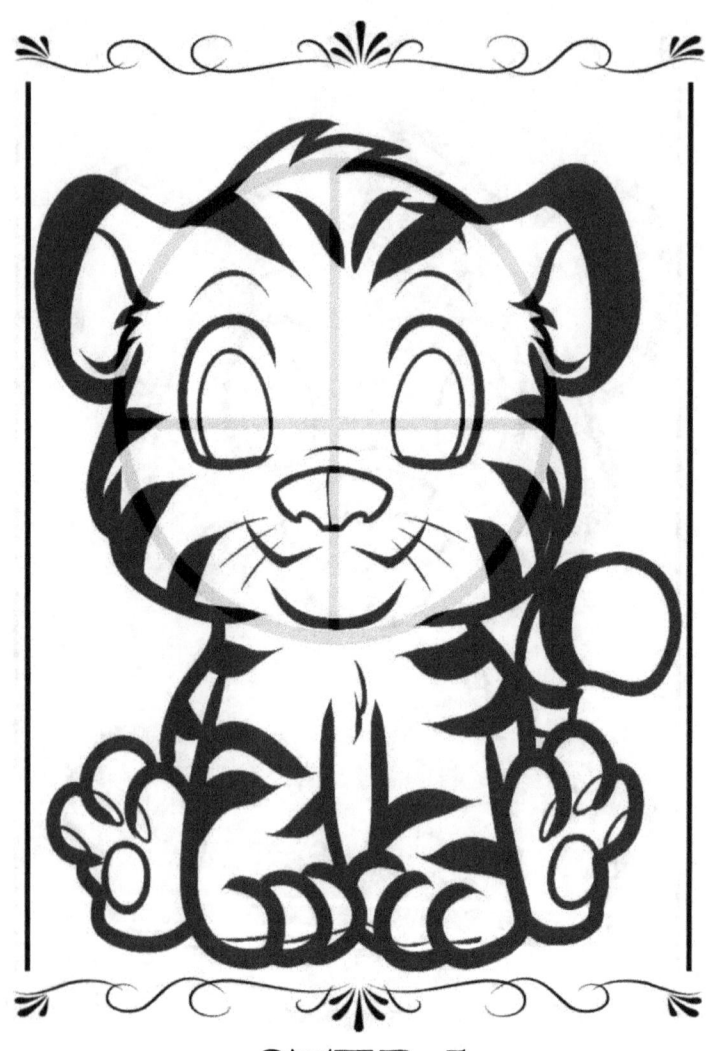

STEP 5

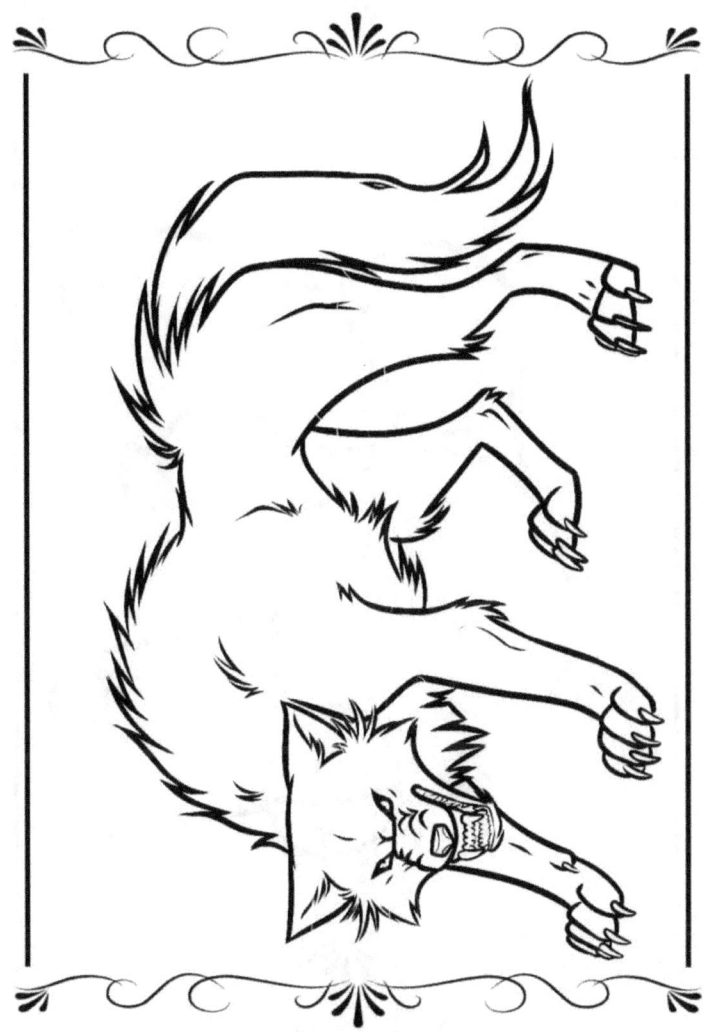

WHITE WOLF

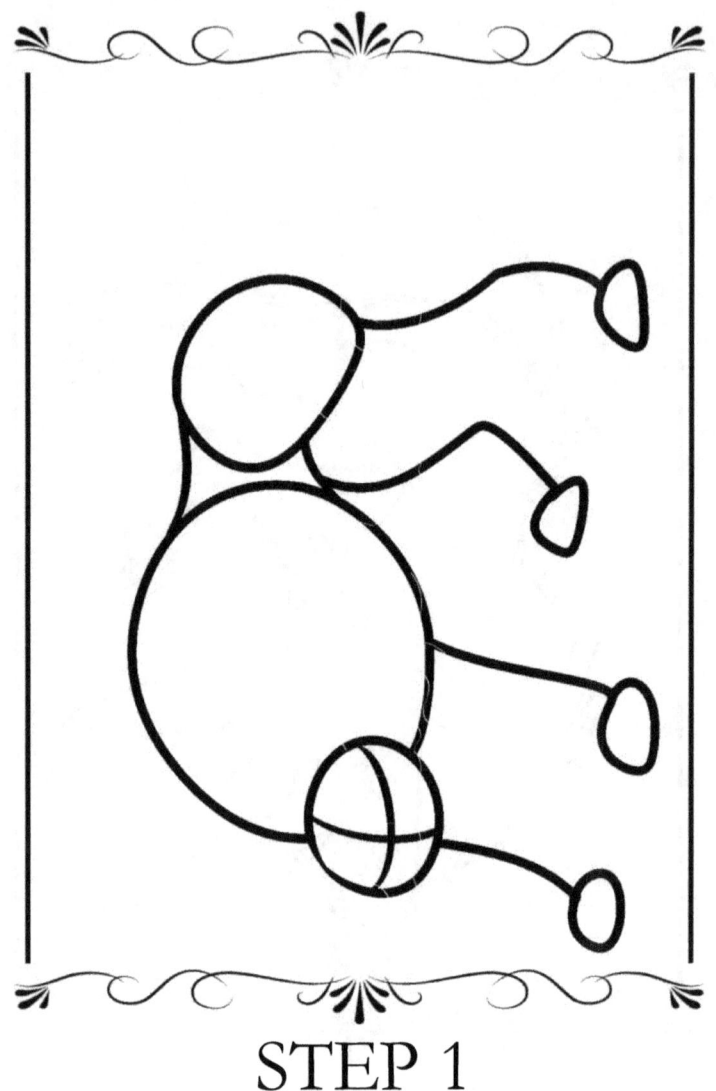

STEP 1

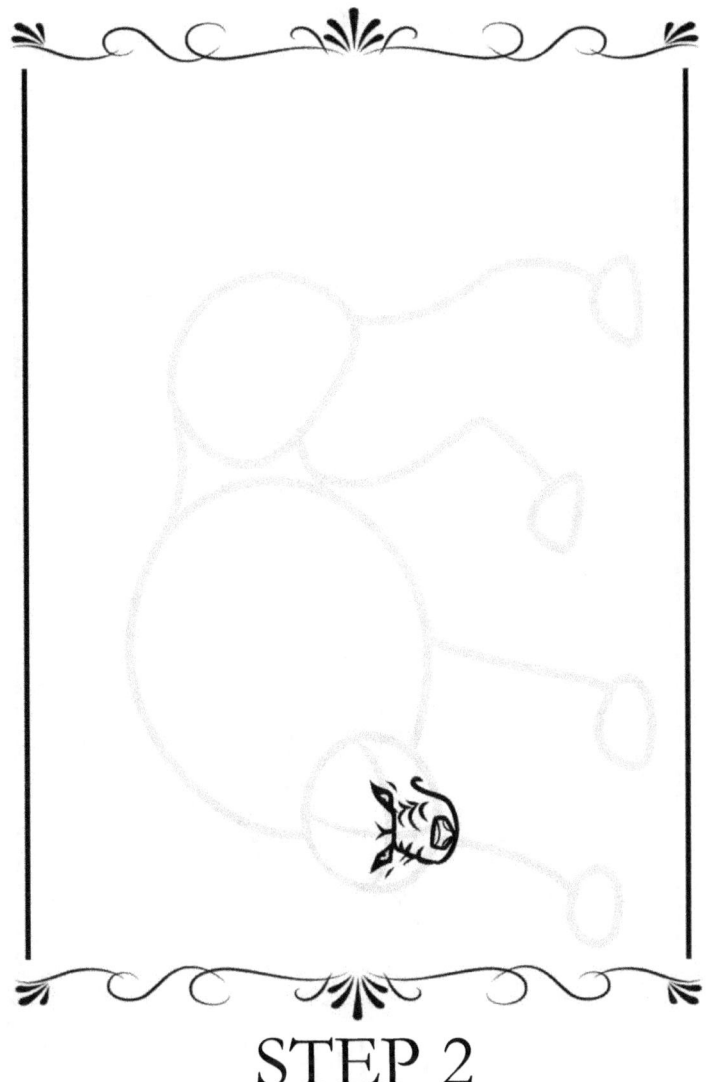

STEP 2

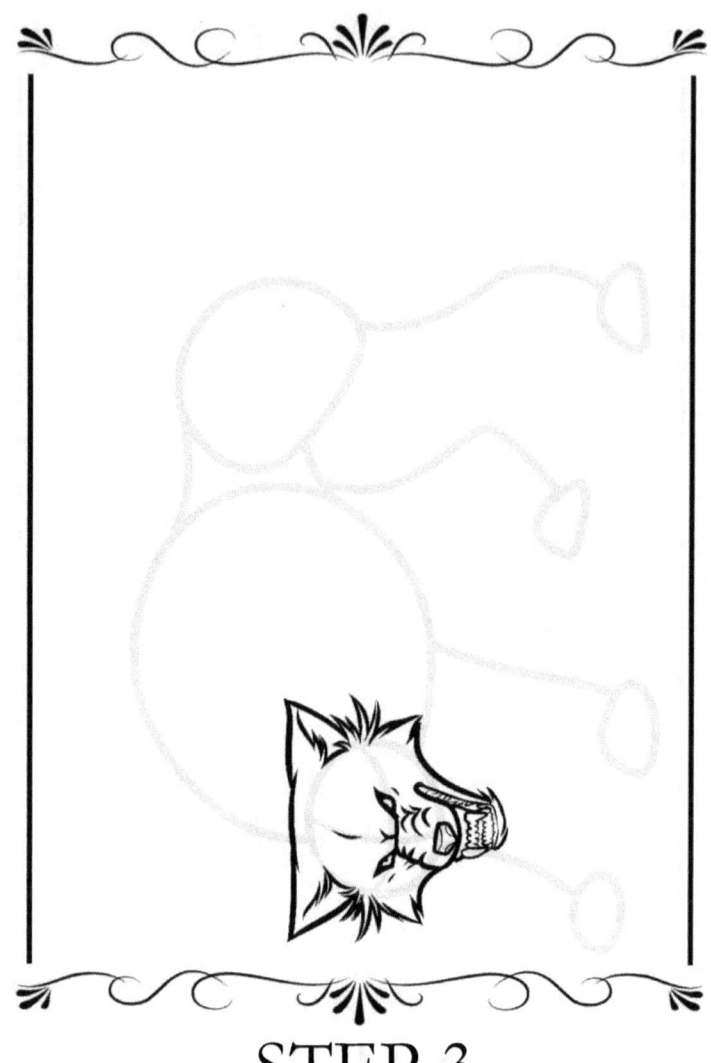

STEP 3

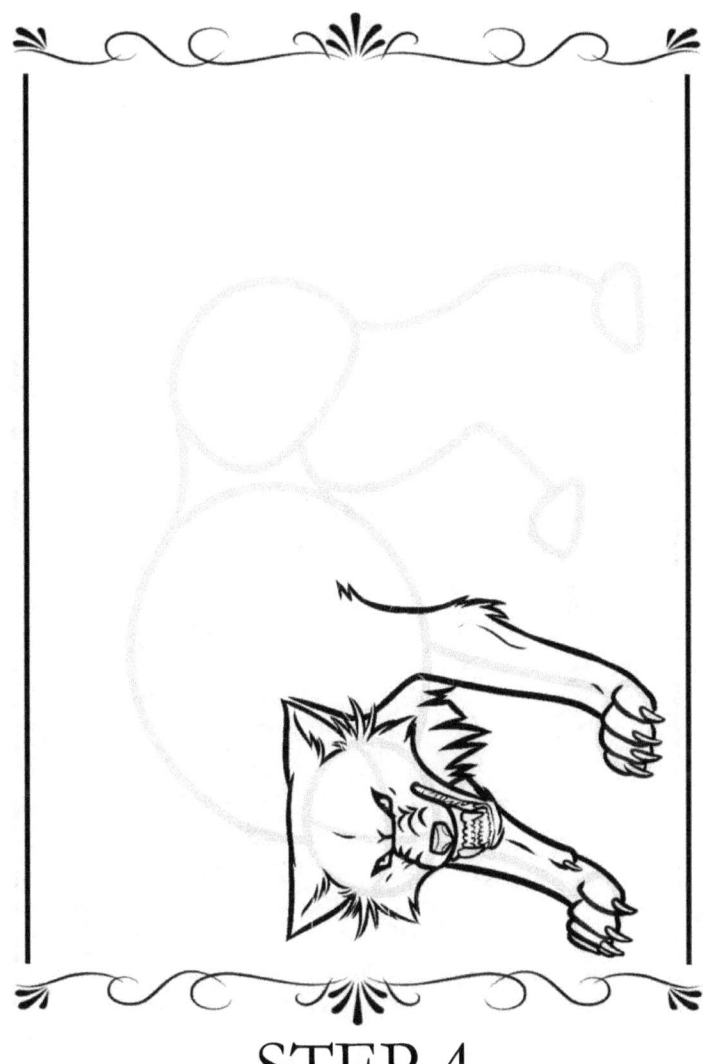

STEP 4

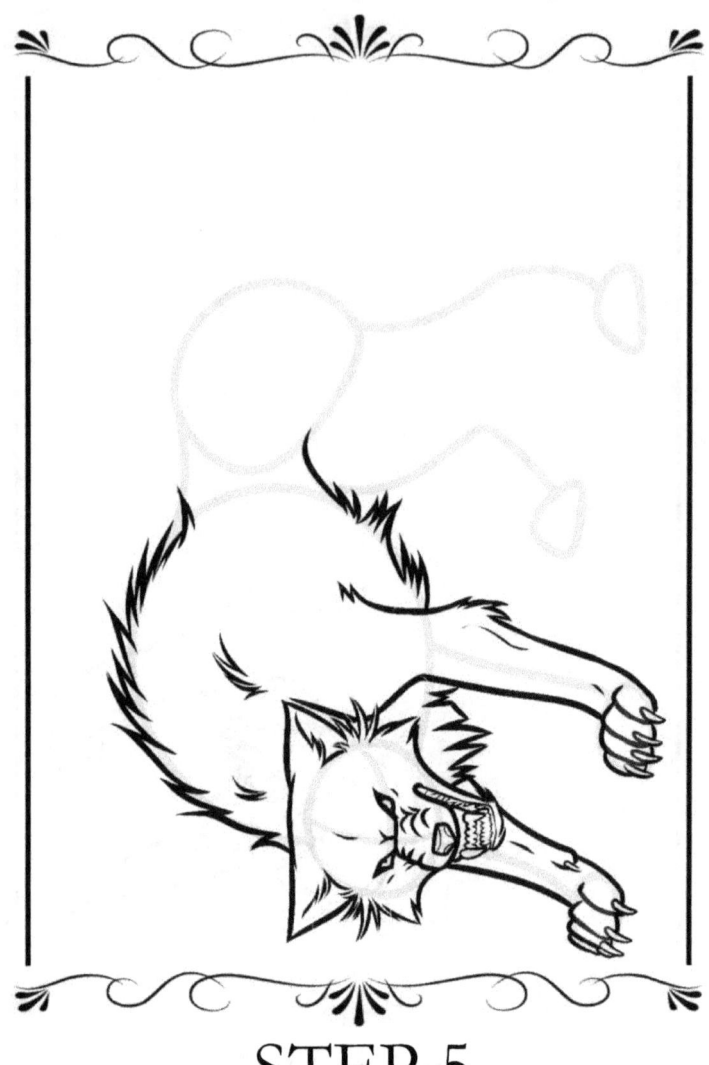

STEP 5

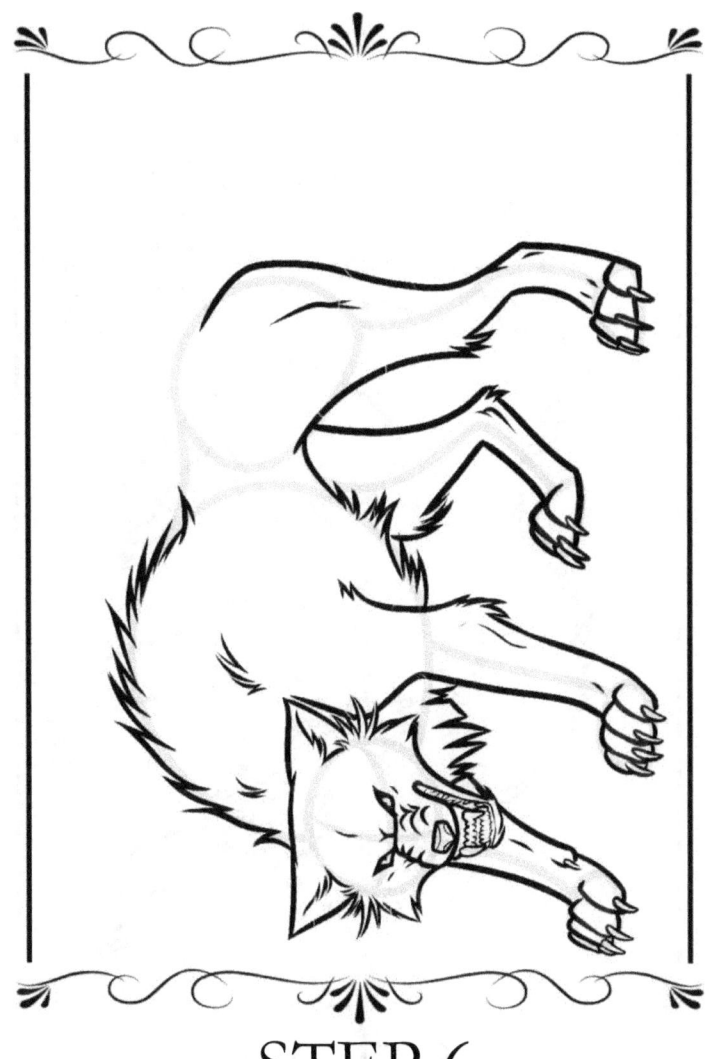

STEP 6

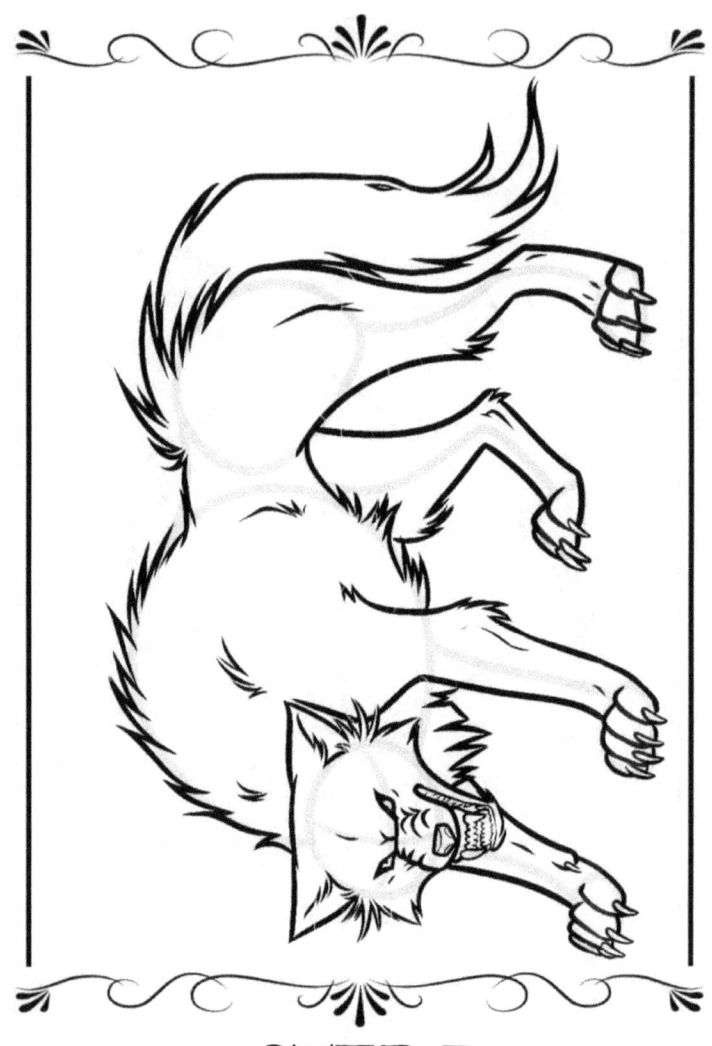

STEP 7

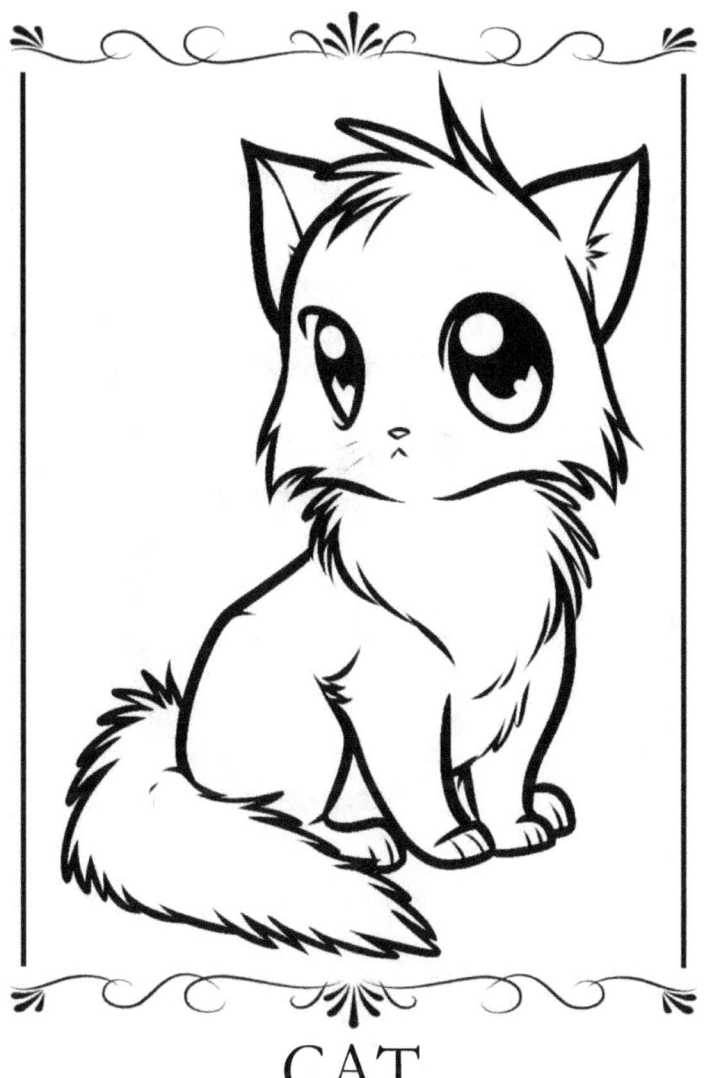

CAT

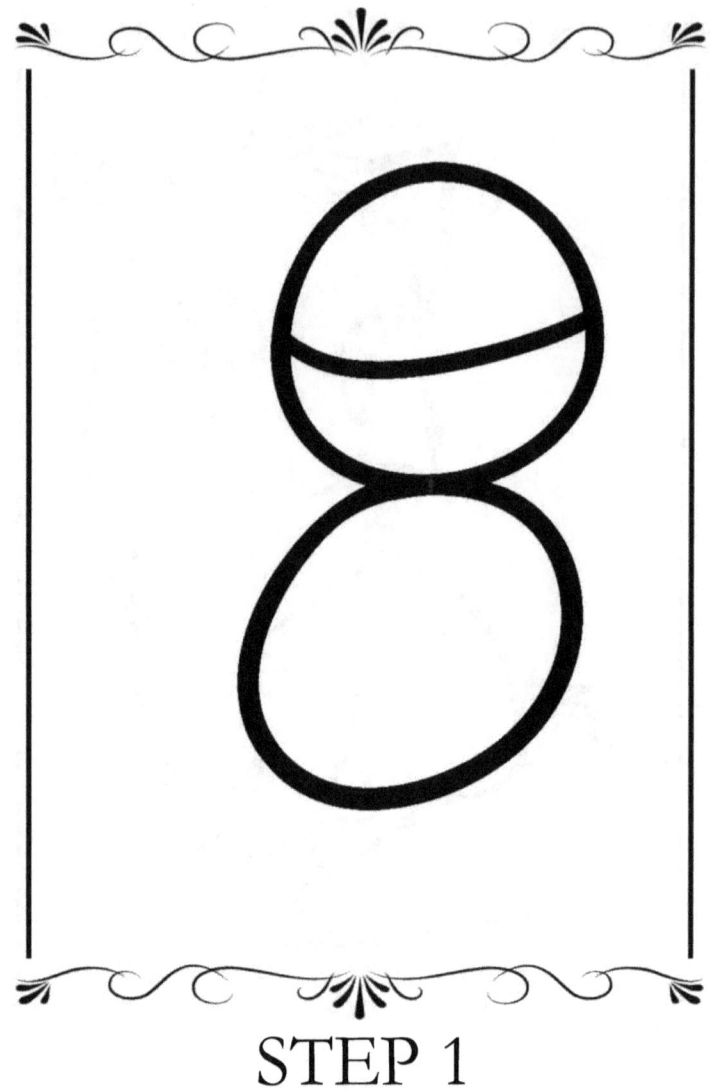

STEP 1

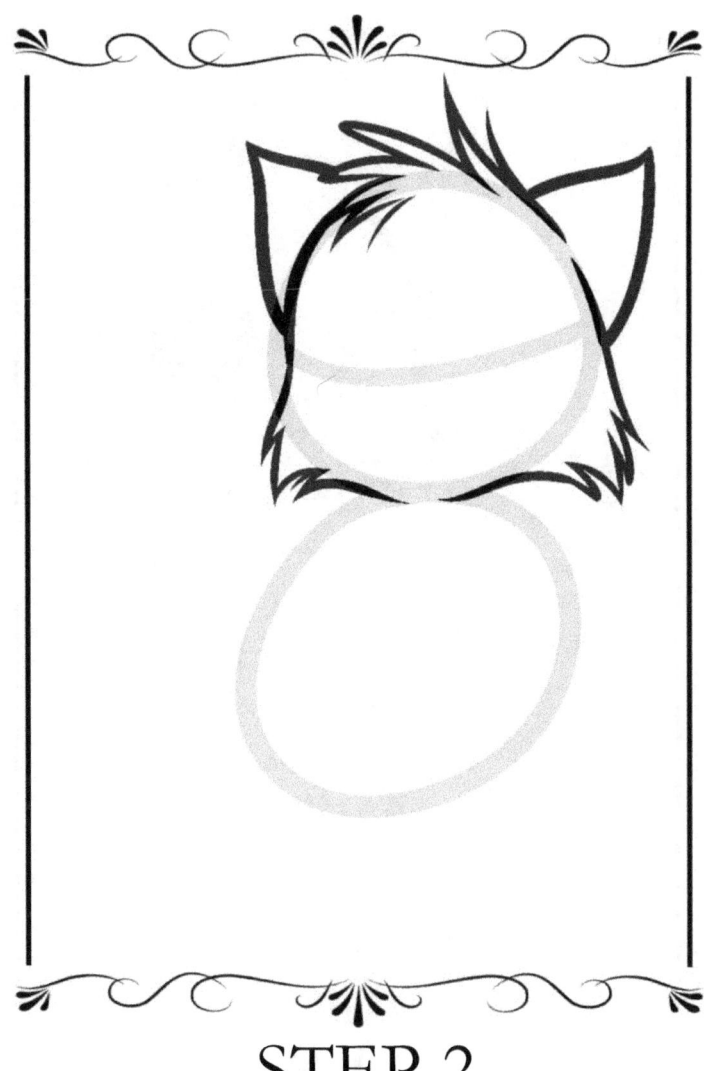

STEP 2

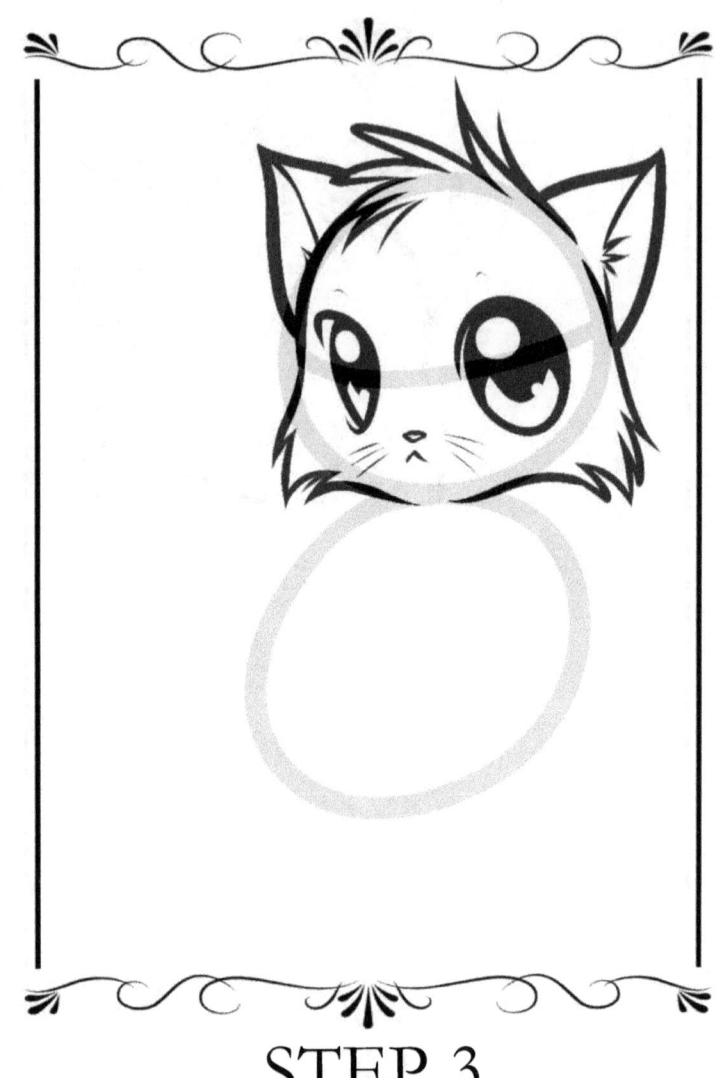

STEP 3

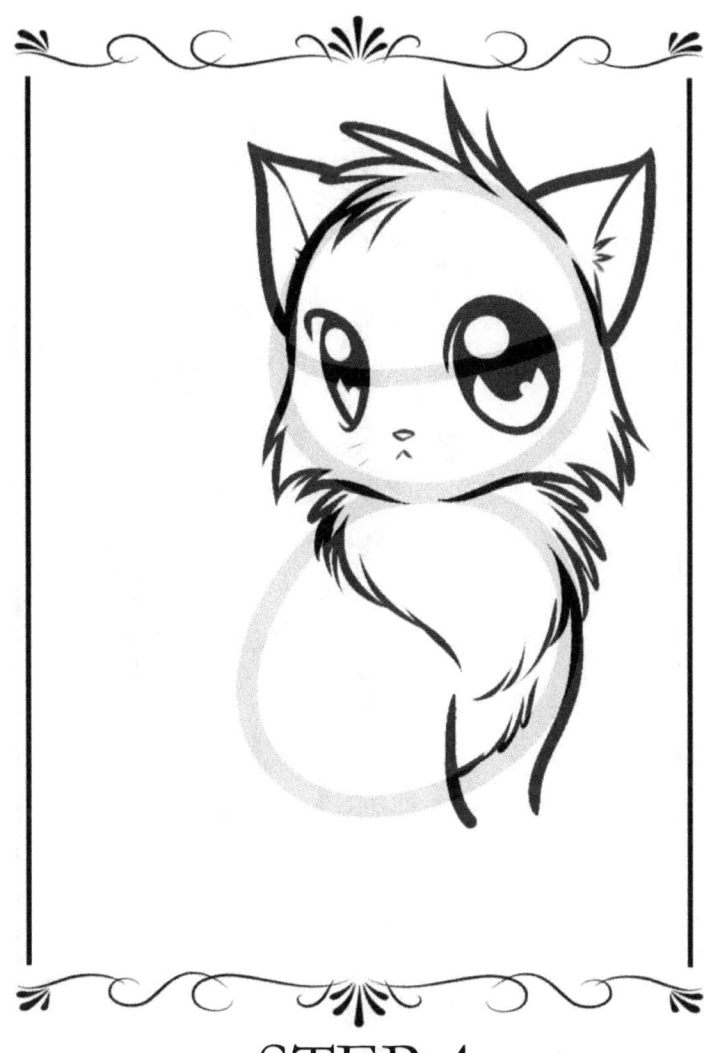

STEP 4

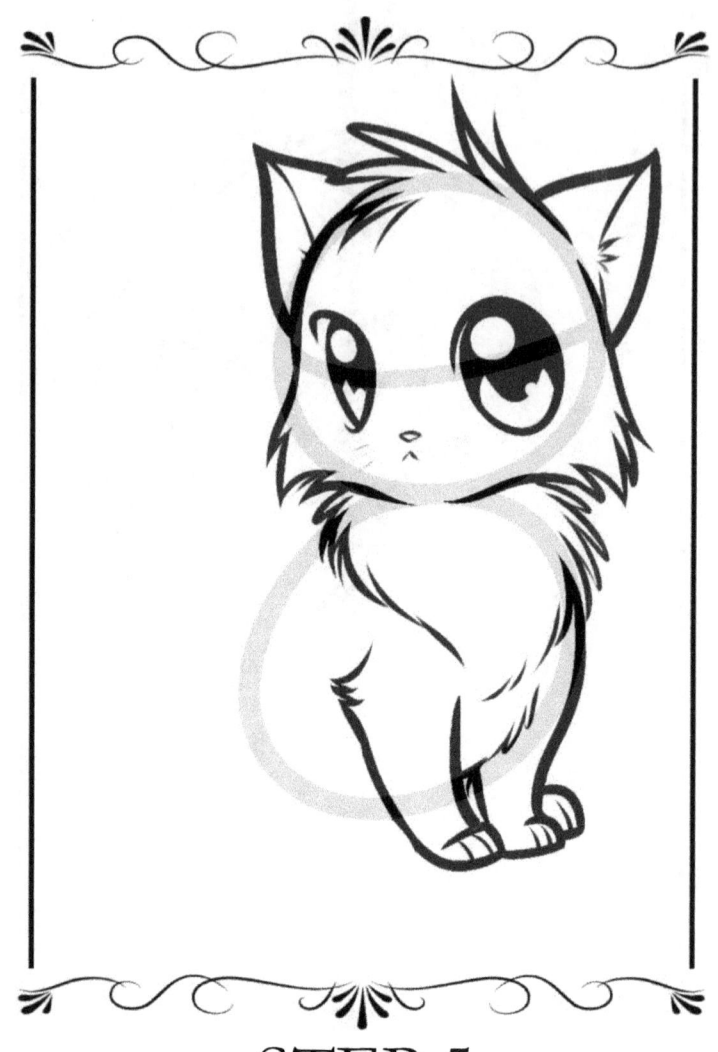

STEP 5

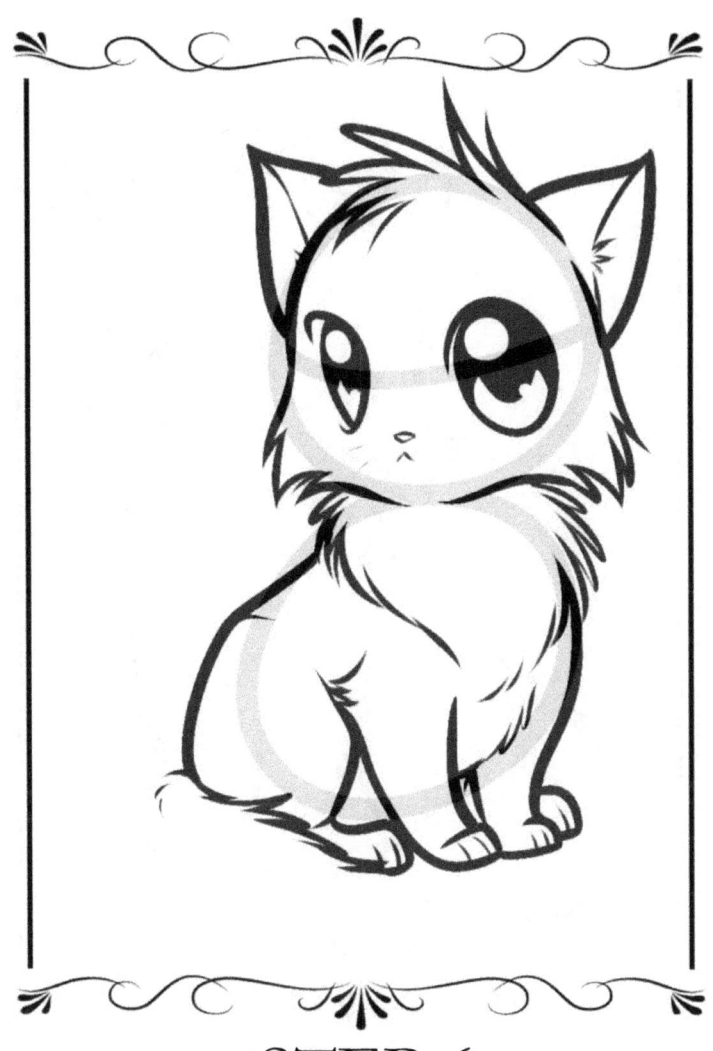

STEP 6

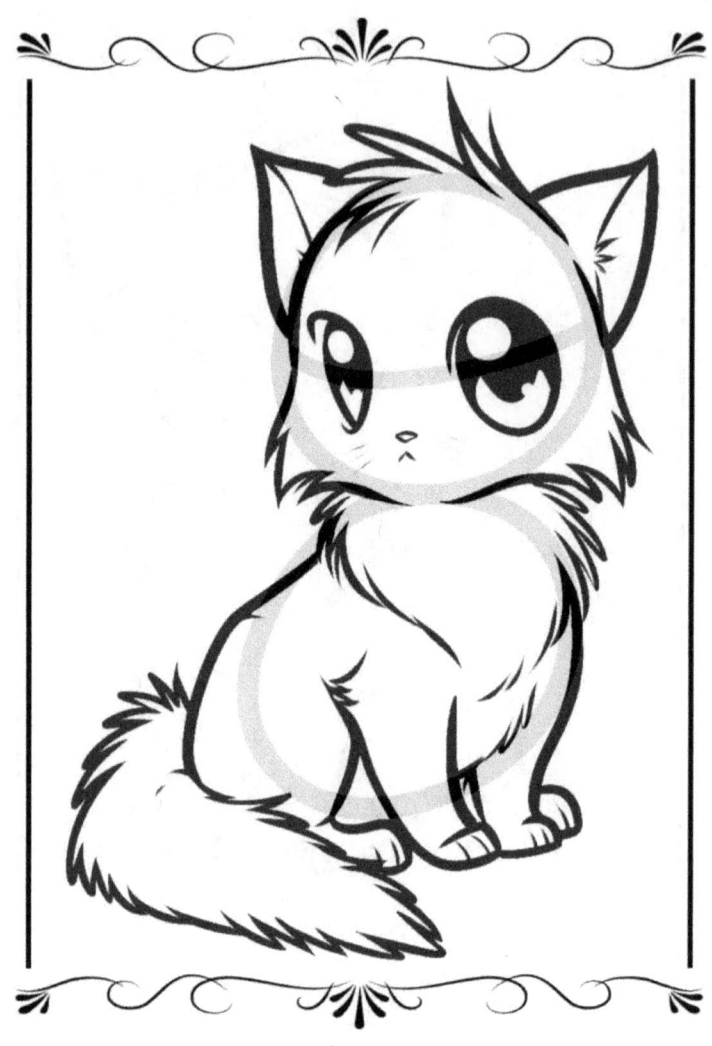

STEP 7

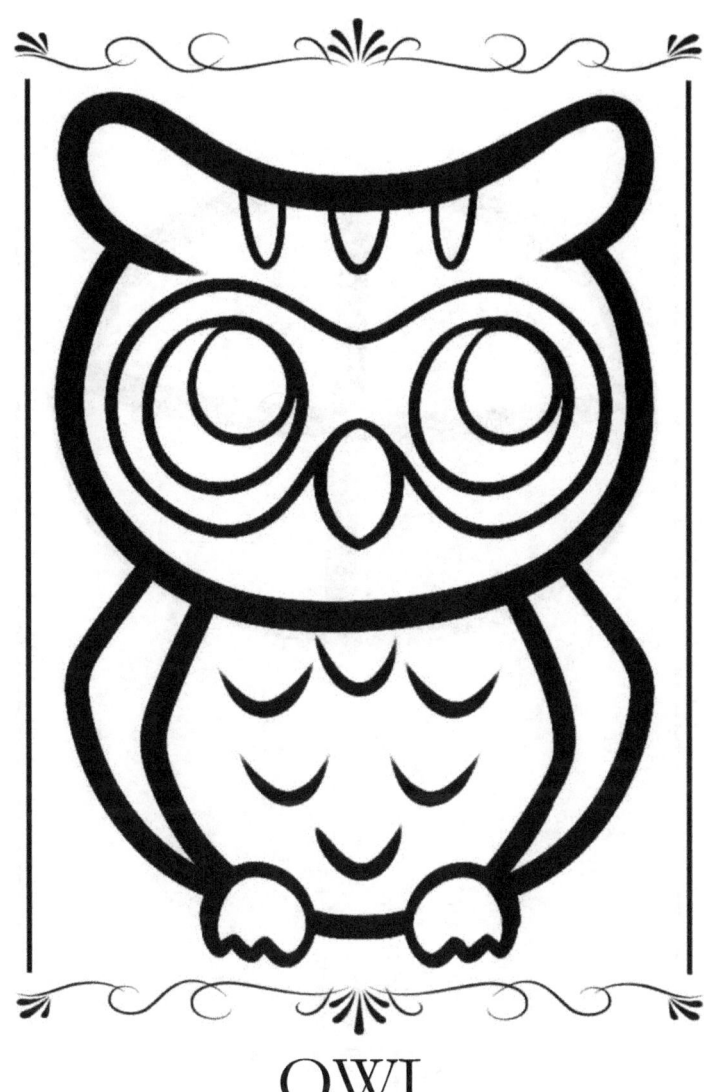

OWL

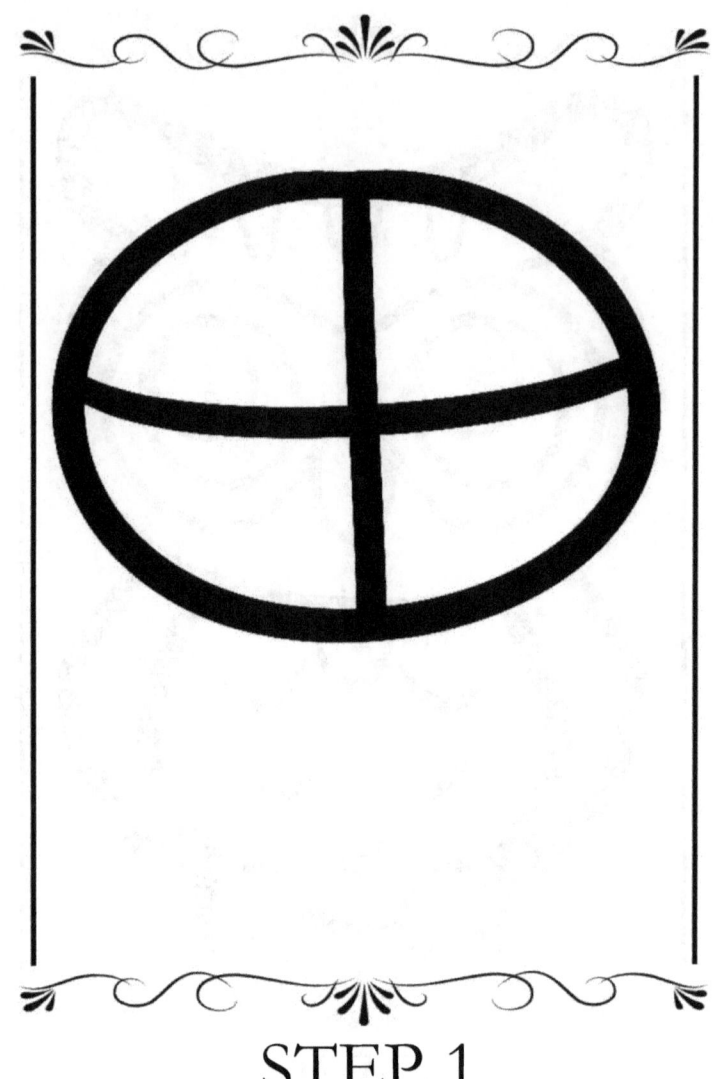

STEP 1

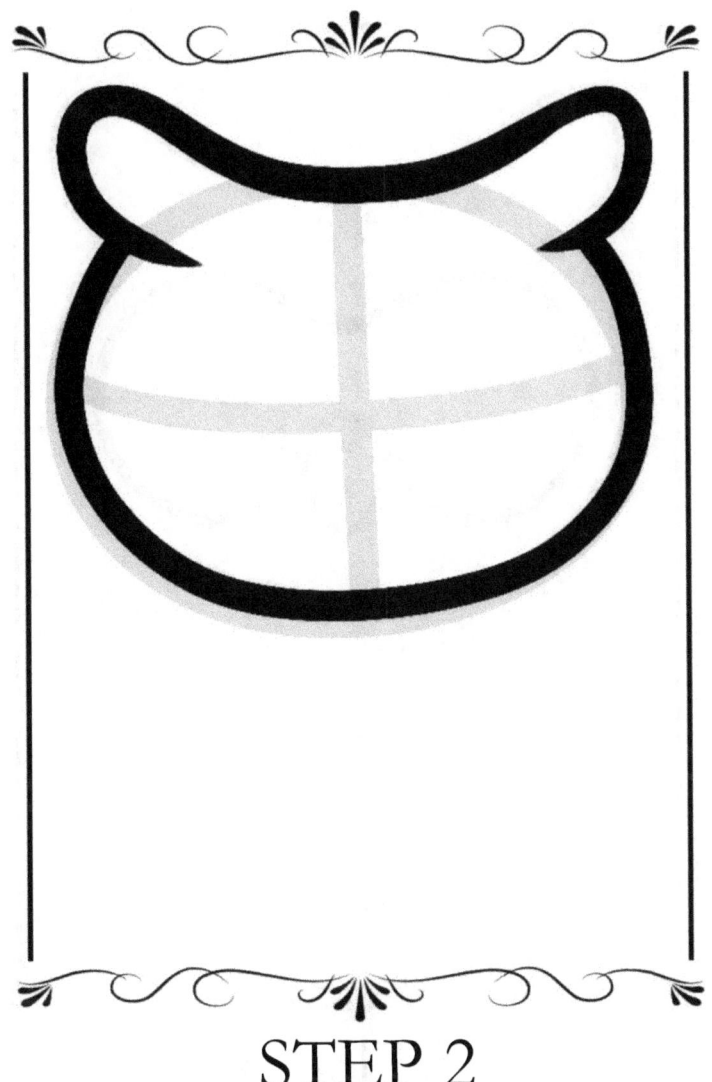

STEP 2

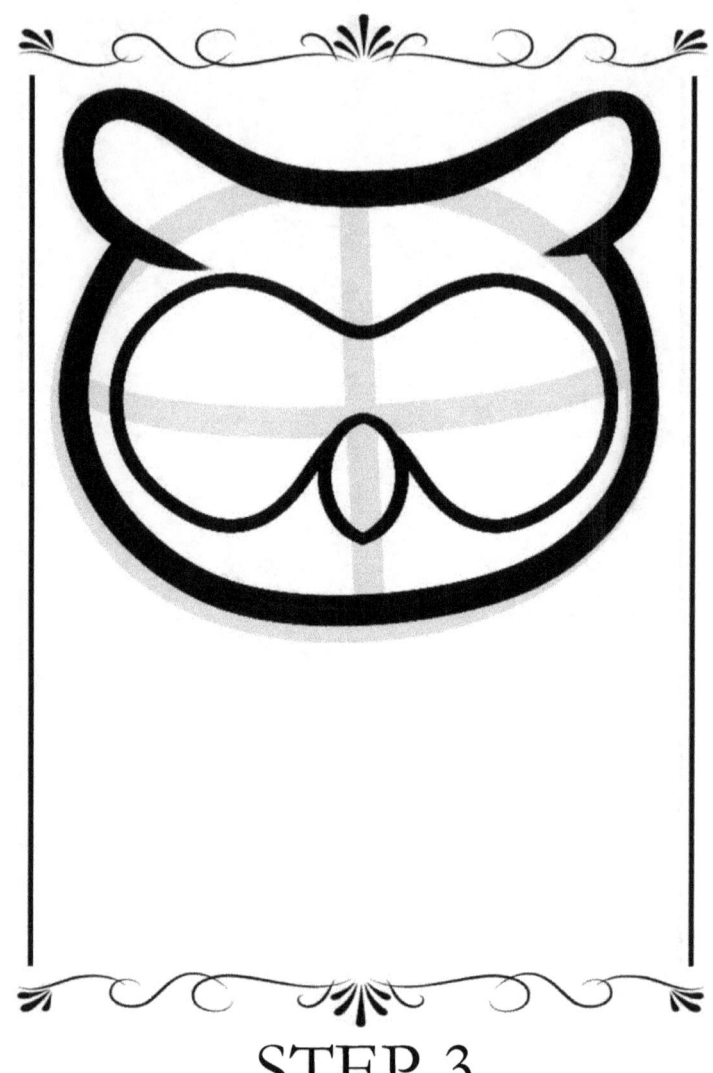

STEP 3

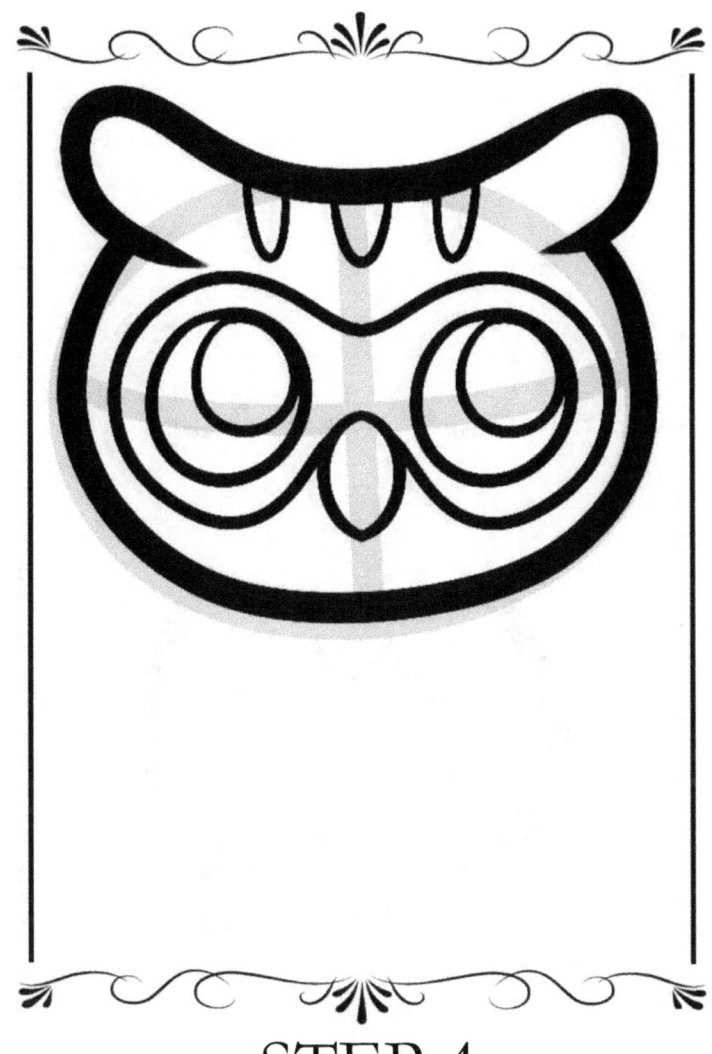

STEP 4

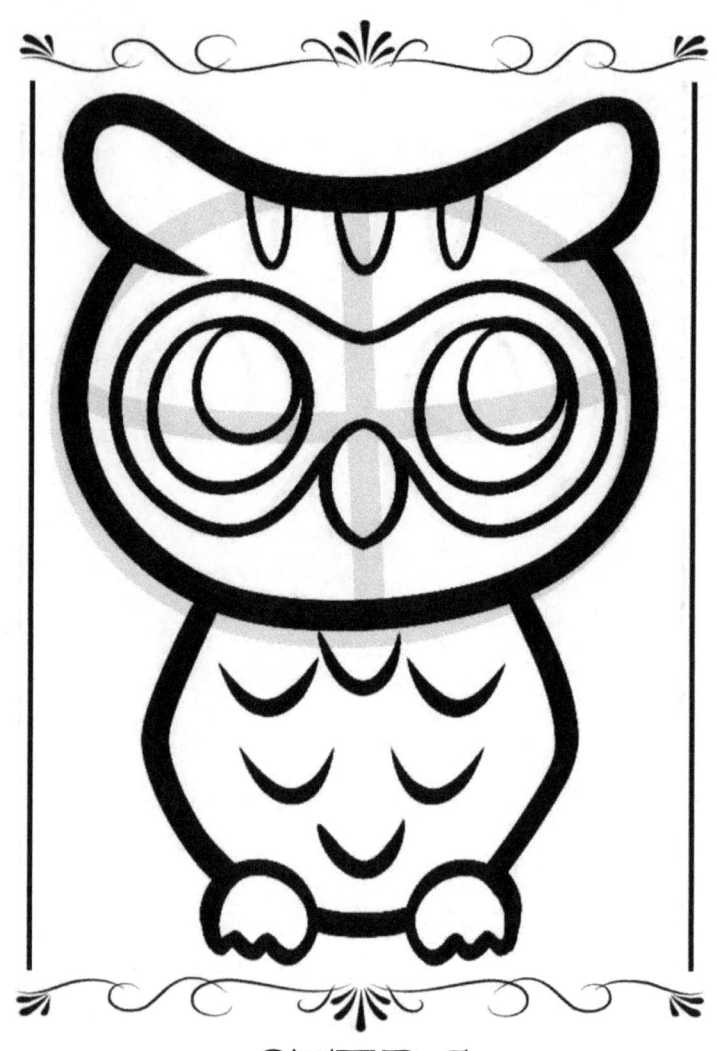

STEP 5

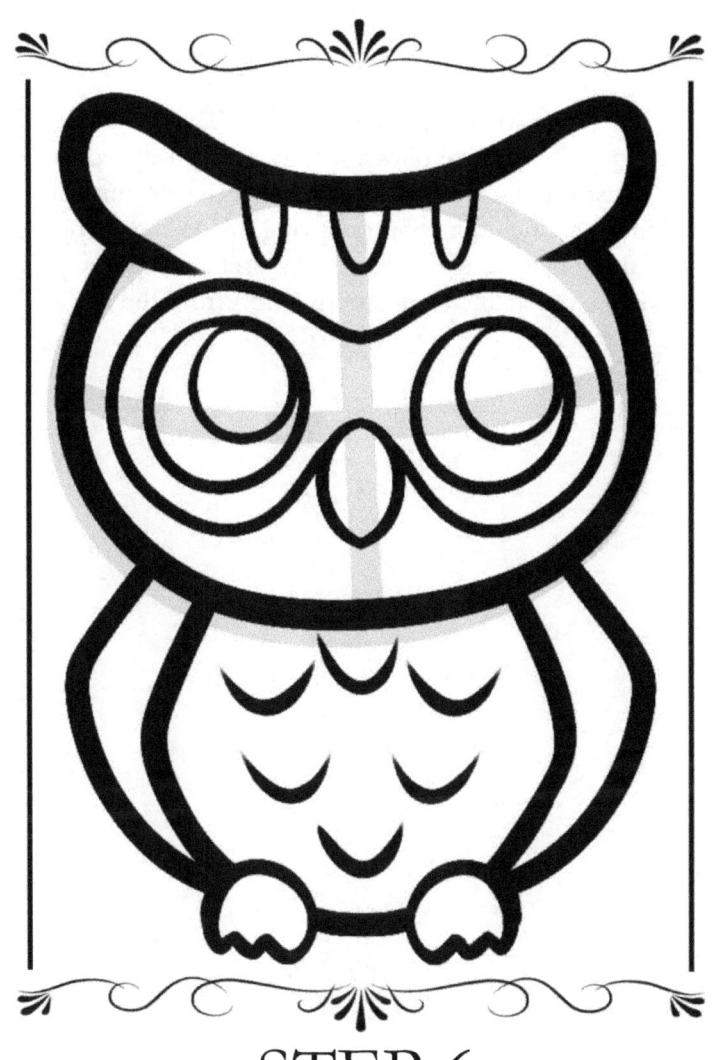

STEP 6

www.ingramcontent.com/pod-product-compliance
Lightning Source LLC
Chambersburg PA
CBHW071649170526
45166CB00003B/1492